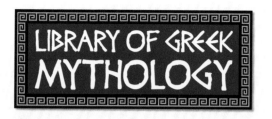

Heroes in Greek Mythology

Don Nardo

ReferencePoint Press®

San Diego, CA

© 2017 ReferencePoint Press, Inc.
Printed in the United States

For more information, contact:
ReferencePoint Press, Inc.
PO Box 27779
San Diego, CA 92198
www.ReferencePointPress.com

LIBRARY OF CONGRESS CATALOGING-IN-PUBLICATION DATA

Names: Nardo, Don, 1947- author.
Title: Heroes in Greek mythology / by Don Nardo.
Description: San Diego : ReferencePoint Press, 2017. | Series: Library of
   Greek mythology series | Includes bibliographical references and index.
Identifiers: LCCN 2015045000 (print) | LCCN 2016006164 (ebook) | ISBN
   9781601529688 (hardback) | ISBN 9781601529695 (epub)
Subjects: LCSH: Heroes--Greece. | Mythology, Greek.
Classification: LCC BL795.H46 N375 2017 (print) | LCC BL795.H46 (ebook) | DDC
   398.20938/02--dc23
LC record available at http://lccn.loc.gov/2015045000

Contents

Ancient Greece (Circa 500 BCE)

Introduction

Tales from the Age of Heroes

He was a mountain of a man—tall, broad shouldered, immensely muscular—and across his mighty chest he wore the skin of a lion he had wrestled and killed with his bare hands. As impressive as these physical attributes were, not immediately visible was his finest feature—the stalwart heart of a hero who fought to protect good people from both injustice and threats to their well-being. His name was Heracles, although in later ages he would become better known as Hercules.

For almost a week he walked through the scenic plains and forests of the central ancient Greek mainland. His challenging mission was to stop a herd of bloodthirsty horses from terrorizing a city in Greece's northernmost region of Thrace. About halfway through his journey he passed near the palace of his friend Admetus, the goodly king of the tiny kingdom of Pherae, and decided to stop for a brief visit. As he approached the palace's front gate, Heracles was disturbed to hear people sobbing loudly inside and wondered what could be causing this commotion.

Entering, the strongman found to his dismay that the king's loving wife, Alcestis, had just died. Along with her royal husband, nearly everyone in the palace was overcome with grief and in the midst of mourning her. At any moment, a servant told Heracles, they anticipated that the deity of death, Thanatos, would arrive to take Alcestis's soul to the dismal underworld. That god was scary and invincible, the servant said, so no one dared to try to stop him. Indeed, another person said, Thanatos's heart was as hard as iron. He had "shameless

The hero Heracles, later known as Hercules, wrestles a lion in a scene from Greek mythology. According to this tale, Heracles slew the lion with his bare hands and thereafter wore its skin over his chest.

feelings without pity inside his breast," and he was "hateful even to the deathless gods!"[1]

Hearing this, the highly compassionate Heracles became determined to stop the gruesome god from taking away virtuous Alcestis's soul. "I must rescue her," the man in the lion skin told the servant, and pay the debt of kindness I owe Admetus by returning Alcestis to her own home once more—alive! The black-robed king of the dead will come to drink the blood of victims offered at her tomb. That's where I'll find him. I'll hide there, watch for him, leap out, and spring on him. And once I have my arms locked round his bruised ribs, there's no power on earth that will be able to wrench him free, till he gives her up to me![2]

Sure enough, when the ghastly Thanatos arrived to cruelly claim his latest prize, Heracles was ready. The fearless man leapt up from his hiding place and confronted the shadowy being. Equally bold, the god refused to back away, and so a tremendous struggle ensued, a fight so fierce that everyone in the palace felt its stones shake and sway. All wondered which of the unwavering warriors would prevail in the ongoing fight for a good woman's soul.

In the Distant Past

No one in classical Greece wondered who would win the famous fight between bighearted Heracles and the dreadful Thanatos. They knew Heracles would triumph in the end. From an early age, all classical Greeks learned that exciting tale, along with hundreds of other myths about heroes, gods, and monsters. When employed in a general manner, the term *classical Greeks* denotes Greece's inhabitants from about 700 to 300 BCE. It was the historical period in which they produced a true cultural golden age. Democratic experimentation, literature, and the arts all blossomed as never before. So too did philosophy, science, and crucial military advances, and together these achievements formed the essential underpinnings of what later came to be called Western (European-based) civilization.

To the Greeks, their myths about Heracles and other daring heroes who killed monsters and interacted with the gods

> **WORD ORIGINS**
>
> ### philosophy
>
> In modern life: the study of the reality of existence, wisdom, knowledge, and human values.
>
> In ancient Greece: *sophia*, meaning wisdom or knowledge.

were not simply entertaining stories. In a very real way the residents of classical Greece perceived them as part of their history. Most Greeks were sure that at some point in the distant past Heracles had been a real man—a son whom Zeus, leader of the gods, had produced with a mortal woman. Just as real, the average Greek felt, was the renowned Trojan War, in which an army of Greeks, among them many warriors of heroic stature, had laid siege to the non-Greek city of Troy (in what is now northwestern Turkey).

Clearly, therefore, the Greeks did not realize the true origins of their heroic myths. In large part this was because they did not possess one of the modern world's most important and effective learning tools—the science of archaeology. By systematically digging up and studying ancient artifacts, twentieth-century archaeologists discovered something they found fascinating. The roots of many of the characters and events in the Greek myths lay within the very real world of a previous Greek society, one that the classical Greeks had no idea existed. That earlier civilization rose and fell during what modern scholars call the late Greek Bronze Age, lasting from about 1600 to 1100 BCE. (The term *bronze* here indicates that at the time people used tools and weapons made of bronze, a mixture of copper and tin.)

The Process of Mythmaking

The archaeologists found that two distinct peoples occupied Greece in the late Bronze Age, viewed by the classical Greeks as the supernatural, adventure-filled Age of Heroes. One of those peoples, the Minoans, who resided on the large Greek island of Crete and nearby Aegean islands, built large structures that functioned as palaces, religious temples, and food-distribution centers. They also carried on a flourishing trade with foreign kingdoms as far away as Egypt.

Minoan cargo ships, and possibly warships too, also made regular trips to the nearby Greek mainland, where the second group of late Bronze Age Greeks dwelled. Dubbed the *Mycenaeans* by modern scholars, they erected small but powerful kingdoms in the Peloponnesus, the big peninsula that makes up the southern third of the mainland. They also had a kingdom centered at Athens, situated farther to the northeast, which would centuries later become Greece's leading political state.

Sometime around 1400 BCE, the Mycenaeans overran the Minoans' population centers in the islands and took over their foreign trade routes as well. For two centuries the mainlanders held sway in the region. But their reign came to a fairly sudden end sometime between 1200 and 1100 BCE, when their society largely collapsed. Modern scholars still debate the reasons for this catastrophe. Archaeologists John Camp and Elizabeth Fisher comment that "the huge palaces with their great circuit walls" were abandoned and "gone also were most indicators of wealth," including luxury items made of gold and silver, along with wall-painting, sculpture, reading, and writing skills. "In place of the palaces were tiny, unfortified settlements with a handful of small houses built with rubble walls and mud, a poor and uninspired repertory [assortment] of pottery, no luxury goods, and a subsistence economy."[3]

In the period that followed, which modern experts call Greece's Dark Age (ca. 1100 to 800 BCE), poverty remained widespread, and over time the illiterate populace largely lost contact with its own past. Some memories of the prior civilization survived, yet they became increasingly exaggerated as they passed from one generation to another by word of mouth. Roving minstrels called bards told and retold the stories of past events, reshaping and embellishing them at will. In this process of mythmaking, some historians say, a number of real Bronze Age individuals were inflated into heroes of tremendous prowess. Similarly, the memory of a successful Mycenaean raid on the rich trading city of Troy was likely overblown into an epic ten-year-long siege in which larger-than-life heroes from both sides clashed. Thus, New York University scholar Philip Mayerson explains, "behind these heroic legends are specks or motes of historical fact, the residue of a long period of oral transmission. In the course of being handed down from father to son and from bard to bard, the dry data of history, such as political, social, and economic factors, were turned into the fascinating stories which have survived to this day."[4]

Bards and Other Myth-Tellers

Therefore, when Greece's Dark Age ended in the early 700s BCE and a new Greek society began to emerge, its members had at their disposal a hefty heap of myths. Many featured heroes of great stature, like Heracles, Achilles, Hector, Odysseus, Theseus, Perseus, and Jason. Over time bards continued to tell and retell their stories, making them literal household names in classical Greece and later in the modern world.

By far the most renowned of the post–Dark Age myth-tellers was Homer, about whose life almost nothing is known. It appears that he inherited two large-scale myths from earlier bards—one about the Trojan War, the other about the adventures of the Greek king Odysseus directly following that conflict. Homer likely added details to and refined the wording of those tales of towering heroes and their illustrious deeds. The result was the *Iliad* and the *Odyssey,* which are considered Western civilization's first and perhaps greatest pieces of literature.

Other Greek and eventually Roman myth-tellers and writers later perpetuated the Greek myths about heroes. Among many others, they included Hesiod (seventh century BCE); Herodotus, Pindar, Aeschylus, Sophocles, Euripides, and Aristophanes (all fifth century BCE); Apollonius of Rhodes (fourth century BCE); Ovid (first century BCE); and Apollodorus (second century CE).

These poets, playwrights, and other writers shaped and defined mythical heroes for all later ages, peoples, and cultures. The concept of the hero *had* existed before the Greeks came on the scene. But in describing their ancient heroes, the Greeks perfected that concept, clarifying it and making it universal. The Greek myths also differentiated various *kinds* of heroes for later generations. Some, like Achilles and Hector, were great warriors who shone on the battlefield. Heroes like Cadmus and Theseus founded new nations. Others, like Jason and Odysseus, journeyed to the ends of the earth on epic quests. And still others, like Heracles and Perseus, confronted and killed terrifying monsters. One crucial distinction these heroic characters share is that they remain as popular today as they were among the classical Greeks who idolized them.

┛┗┛┗┛┗┛┗┛┗┛┗┛┗┛┗┛┗┛┗┛┗┛┗┛┗┛┗┛┗┛┗

Chapter One

Champions of the Trojan War

More than most peoples in history, the classical Greeks idolized their mythical heroes, and in Greek eyes the most admirable heroes of all were those who fought in the Trojan War. Indeed, that legendary conflict seemed the perfect venue for a heroic champion to prove himself. To understand why the Greeks saw it this way, one only has to consider their definition of a mythical hero and how they viewed that war, which remains universally famous today.

To the Greeks, the heroes of their myths were larger-than-life figures who possessed extraordinary abilities, such as superhuman strength, endurance, courage, and cunning. Such talents allowed a hero to accomplish deeds that everyday people could not. For instance, the Greek mythical heroes typically killed frightening monsters, overthrew tyrants who oppressed their subjects, and rescued individuals from dangerous situations and injustice.

The most impressive and praiseworthy heroes of all, however, were warriors with incomparable military skills who lacked *phobos*, or "fear," and proved themselves superior fighters on the battlefield.

WORD ORIGINS

phobos

In ancient Greece: fear.

In modern life: a phobia, meaning an intense fear that a person feels for an object, place, or situation.

The warrior hero also possessed honor and integrity in the highest degree and was willing to die to maintain it. Indeed, death itself was

┛┗┛┗┛┗┛┗┛┗┛┗┛┗┛┗┛┗┛┗┛┗┛┗┛┗┛┗┛┗┛┗

key because the Greek heroic ideal envisioned dying in battle as the ultimate honor and the basis of true and worthy fame.

Homer expressed this heroic concept perfectly in his epic of the Trojan War, the *Iliad*. At one point, the war's greatest hero, Achilles, a man obsessed with gaining military fame, states, "If I stay here and fight and die at Troy, my glory will last forever." In contrast, "if I go home to my fatherland, I will live a long life, but my great reputation will not live on."[5]

Homer's works and the heroic ideals expressed in them had a profound effect on Greek thinking and society. The *demos*, or "people," of each classical city-state viewed the *Iliad* as a sort of Greek international epic. (The city-states, each a political unit built around a central town, viewed themselves as independent nations within the Greek-speaking world.)

Moreover, the Trojan War was widely seen as the model for all wars. Likewise, its heroes were the classic models for any and all Greek soldiers who sought victory and honor in battle. In the words of the late great scholar C.M. Bowra, the Greeks viewed many of the warriors of the Trojan War as "a race of supermen, of heroes who were endowed physically and mentally beyond the common lot and who lived for action and the glory which it brings, especially through prowess in battle."[6]

Inspired by the War at Troy

Partly as a result of these facts, the classical Greeks saw war as a regular, necessary part of life and had many military and social customs built around the idea of violent death in wartime. Perhaps the most renowned example of a Greek custom that equated both victory and death on the battlefield with heroism and honor was quoted by the first-century CE Greek biographer Plutarch. Speaking of Sparta, the most militaristic classical Greek state, he recorded an old adage attributed to Spartan mothers. When a young Spartan man was leaving for war, his mother handed him his shield and said, "Son, either with this or on it."[7] That is, the son should either return from a victory proudly carrying his shield or return from a defeat lying dead on the shield, proof that he had died trying to achieve honor.

To come home alive from a defeat was therefore seen as dishonorable, at least in classical Sparta. Not all Greeks were as fanatical about life and death in battle as Spartan society seems to have been. Yet all were no less moved and inspired as the Spartans were by the heroic actions of Achilles and the other champions of the siege of Troy.

In the original tale, the trouble began when a Trojan prince named Paris arrived in Sparta, located in the southern Peloponnesus, on a diplomatic mission. He subsequently ran away with the queen, the famously beautiful Helen. Her husband, King Menelaus, appealed to his brother, Agamemnon, ruler of Mycenae (in the northeastern Peloponnesus). Agamemnon then rallied several other Greek kings who each brought soldiers to Troy, where the united Greek army besieged the city for ten years. In the end, it fell, Menelaus got Helen back, and most surviving Trojans were reduced to slavery.

Contrary to a common misconception, the many myths making up this complex story do not all appear in Homer's *Iliad*. That great work deals with a series of episodes in the siege's final year and ends before Troy's fall. Yet Homer's epic does zero in on the leading Greek hero, Achilles, and his interactions with the war's other major heroic characters.

Achilles Goes to War

Achilles was the chief archetype, or classic example, of the mythical Greek military hero. One factor in his favor from the start was that he possessed some divine blood, as his mother was a nymph (minor nature goddess) named Thetis, who had mated with a human—Peleus, ruler of the small Greek kingdom of Phthia. One myth claimed that Thetis dipped her newborn son in the Styx, the murky river that ran along the border of the underworld. It was said that this made his body secure from injury, except for the heel by which she held him.

Another way that Thetis tried to ensure her son's safety was to consult an oracle, a priestess who it was thought had the ability to relay

Thetis, the mother of the warrior Achilles, gives her son a shield in preparation for battle. In Spartan society, a soldier was expected to return from war victoriously carrying his shield or lying dead on it after a defeat. To return from a defeat alive was considered dishonorable.

messages from the *theoi*, or "gods," to humans. The oracle predicted that if Achilles fought in a war he would be killed and die young. It is not surprising, therefore, that when the Greeks began gathering at the port town of Aulis for the expedition to Troy, Thetis became fearful.

Once more hoping to protect her son from harm, "Thetis sent the young hero to stay with his uncle, who was bidden to disguise him in women's clothes," modern mythologist Max J. Herzberg writes. However, another hero, Odysseus, king of the island kingdom of Ithaca, tracked Achilles down. Known for his cleverness, Odysseus dressed himself as a merchant and managed to get inside the uncle's house. "On his trays," Herzberg continues, "were many articles such as appeal to women, but mingled with them were a sword and a buckler [small round shield]. As he spread out his wares before the royal maidens, he noticed that one of them disregarded the ribbons and the linens and fingered the sword eagerly. So he discovered Achilles, and in a little while he persuaded him to accompany him back to Aulis."[8]

During the initial years of the Greeks' siege of Troy, Achilles fought fiercely and proved an inspiration to his fellow warriors. During the tenth year of the war, however, according to Homer, he squabbled with the overall Greek commander, Agamemnon, over a woman. Achilles became so upset that he stormed off to his tent and refused to fight unless he got his way. Losing their finest warrior demoralized the Greek fighters. As a result, the Trojans began to make headway and pushed the Greeks back to the beach, where their camp and ships were located.

Worried, Achilles's close friend Patroclus pleaded with him to reenter the fray. But Achilles refused to budge. Hoping to turn things around for the Greeks, Patroclus hatched a daring plan. He sneaked away with his friend's distinctive armor, put it on, and hurried into the battle still raging near the beach. Assuming that Achilles was back in the fight, the Greeks took heart and pushed the Trojans back onto the flat plain stretching before the city.

At that point, Hector, Troy's most formidable warrior hero, decided he must eliminate Achilles. Furiously rushing forward, Hector met and killed Patroclus in single combat as soldiers from both sides watched. The victor did not realize he had slain the wrong person until he yanked off the dead man's helmet.

When the news of Patroclus's death reached the real Achilles, the latter became a changed man. Leaping to his feat, he charged into the battle and led the Greeks in a tremendous offensive that

WORD ORIGINS

theoi

In ancient Greece: the gods.

In modern life: theology, the study of the nature of god and religion.

pushed the Trojans back behind their city's walls. Only brave Hector remained behind. Resolutely, he stood alone on the plain, clearly challenging Achilles to step out and meet him in single combat.

The Influences of Mythical Warfare

The one-on-one combats between Hector and Patroclus and Achilles and Hector were only two of several examples of that sort of fighting that Homer describes in the *Iliad.* Modern experts have long debated how these mythical duels either influenced or reflected real warfare among the Greeks. Some evidence suggests that such contests were fairly common in Bronze Age warfare. It appears that the leading warriors—like the mythical heroes Homer described—employed chariots. Actual chariot battles involving masses of those vehicles were rare and on the small side. This is because Greece is quite mountainous and has few open plains that would make large-scale chariot warfare practical.

Instead, those early Greek champions used their chariots like taxis to ride out onto the battlefield and then climbed down to fight on foot. It appears that sometimes a representative from each side met in a two-man duel, like those Homer depicts, while soldiers from the two armies watched. Some idea of what such a fight was like is well illustrated by the legendary duel between Achilles and Hector. When they met before Troy's towering walls, Achilles jumped from his chariot and the two circled each other, brandishing their primary weapon—the bronze-tipped spear. The object was to thrust that weapon into an eye, the throat, or some other momentarily exposed spot on the opponent's body. In Homer's words, Achilles

> examined Hector with a hardened heart, searching for a spot on the man's body where he could strike a blow. Hector was well-protected by the excellent armor he had taken off Patroclus, yet an open spot was visible in the lower-neck area—the throat where a strike causes a swift death. Achilles aimed for that spot and his spear-point penetrated the neck, making Hector collapse into the dirt. [Then] Achilles jubilantly yelled, "I have beaten you! Now your body will be picked apart by dogs and birds!"[9]

Achilles stabs Hector in the throat in a scene described in the Iliad. *A duel like this one would have been carried out during war by a representative from each side while soldiers from the two's respective armies watched.*

It is unknown whether such duels between two opposing champions continued to supplement clashes between large groups of soldiers past the close of the Bronze Age. Also, exactly how those early Greek armies fought is unclear. What is more certain is that by the advent of the classical age two-man duels had been abandoned. Moreover, a new military system appeared in the 700s BCE in which the soldiers in a

Myth-Tellers' Corner: Homer

The classical Greeks admired the bard Homer so much that they referred to him, often with a touch of awe and even reverence, as "the poet." Modern scholars are fairly certain that he lived sometime between 800 and 650 BCE. They also agree that his seminal accomplishment was his work on two existing epic poems that had been circulated by other bards for at least a century or two before his birth. One, the *Iliad,* depicts several key characters and events from the Trojan War. The other, the *Odyssey,* follows the hero Odysseus during his ten years of wandering after the close of that conflict. It appears that the pre-Homeric bards recited these tales from memory, each adding a few new details. In this way, the poems grew longer over time. Homer made the most extensive additions, and it was his version that was finally written down during the 500s BCE.

The many separate myths contained within Homer's epics profoundly affected classical Greek culture and thought. According to the late historian Michael Grant, the two works formed the foundation of the Greeks'

> literary, artistic, moral, social, educational, and political attitudes. For a long time no histories of early times seemed at all necessary, since the *Iliad* and *Odyssey* fulfilled every requirement. They attracted universal esteem and reverence, too, as sources of general and practical wisdom, as arguments for heroic yet human nobility and dignity, as incentives to vigorous (often warlike) manly action, and as mines of endless quotations and commentaries, the common property of Greeks everywhere.

Michael Grant, *The Rise of the Greeks.* New York: Macmillan, 1987, p. 147.

city-state's army stood in a rigid formation called a phalanx. It was a long block of soldiers standing in ranks (lines), one behind the other, eight ranks being the average depth.

When attacking an enemy force, the men raised their shields and marched forward in unison, creating a great deal of momentum. Then, as two opposing phalanxes came together, they pushed each other back and forth in a sort of gigantic shoving match. Meanwhile, the soldiers in the front ranks jabbed their spears at their opponents.

Although the phalanx system was a product of the early classical era, the influence of the duels described in mythology on the newer type of warfare is stunning. When Greeks fought Greeks in classical times, two phalanxes—each moving as a single unit—performed their own duel, only on a much larger scale than in the two-man variety. Furthermore, the primary weapon remained the thrusting spear, now with an iron rather than bronze tip. The sword each soldier carried was mainly a backup weapon used if he lost or broke his spear. Overall, therefore, the later Greeks fought in what was essentially a larger-scale and much perfected version of the warfare depicted in their myths.

Alexander and Ajax

The heroes of the Trojan War influenced people in classical times in other ways as well. Achilles, for instance, was appealing to many later Greeks not only because of his fighting skills but also because of his outlook on life, death, and fame. In the *Iliad,* soon after Hector's demise, Achilles is slain by Paris. The latter manages to shoot an arrow into his one vulnerable spot—the heel his mother had held him by when he was an infant. Thus, the oracular prophecy Thetis had tried to avert is fulfilled and Achilles gets his wish—to die young and be forever famous rather than die an old man in obscurity.

Of the later Greeks who admired Achilles's view of life and death, the most famous was Alexander III (356–323 BCE), ruler of the kingdom of Macedonia in northern Greece. Better known to history as Alexander the Great, he conquered much of the known world in the final years of the classical age. Achilles was his personal hero. In fact, Alexander, who carried a copy of the *Iliad* with him at all times, saw

Macedonian ruler Alexander the Great, pictured here taming a wild horse, conquered much of the known world toward the end of the classical age. Alexander viewed Achilles as his hero and thought of himself as a latter-day version of his idol.

himself as a latter-day Achilles. The young conqueror believed that, like his idol, he was destined to die young yet to be remembered for-ever. According to Alexander's chief ancient biographer, Arrian, he told his soldiers that "those who endure hardship and danger are the ones who achieve glory; and the most gratifying thing is to live with courage and to die leaving behind eternal renown."[10] True to form, Alexander died at the young age of thirty-two (possibly of alcohol poisoning) and is still widely famous.

Still another concept the classical Greeks absorbed from the stories of long-dead legendary heroes was the importance of personal

Defining the Hero

The concept of the ancient Greek mythical hero has fascinated Western thinkers, scholars, writers, and readers for thousands of years. Many of those observers have attempted to define such a hero but have inevitably found that it is no easy task. The heroic characters in the Greek myths were frequently complex individuals with numerous positive traits and abilities, often along with some flaws and failings as well. Thus, summing them up in a single, short definition is impossible. Exploring their positive features, some writers have pointed out that they were typically stronger, bolder, cleverer, and/or more driven than ordinary people. Also, through a hero's exploits he or she frequently set an example for others to follow. Hopefully he or she inspired them to rise above their mundane natures and surroundings. The noted nineteenth-century teacher, priest, historian, and novelist Charles Kingsley offered more insights about mythical Greek heroes. They were "brave and skillful," he once wrote, "and dared do more than other men." Later, he added that those ancient heroes were

> men who helped their country; men in those old times, when the country was half wild, who killed fierce beasts and evil men, and drained swamps, and founded towns, and therefore after they were dead, were honored, because they had left their country better than they found it. And we call such a man a hero in English to this day, and call it a "heroic" thing to suffer pain and grief, that we may do good to our fellow men.

Charles Kingsley, *The Heroes.* Boston: Ticknor and Fields, 1856, pp. 21–22.

honor. People viewed it as a combination of honesty and following certain set customs in which one showed deference, or respect, to one's peers, often including an opponent or enemy. If a person failed to show proper respect, he or she was seen to have committed a shameful act and might be criticized or even shunned.

Another of the heroes of the Trojan War, Ajax, became a popular model for honorable behavior. Homer and other ancient authors described him as a very large man with immense strength and courage. During the siege of Troy, Ajax often helped his fellow Greeks when they were facing certain death, and he also performed some impressive physical feats. In a personal duel with Hector, for example, the giant picked up an enormous rock no other man could lift and tossed it at his opponent, smashing his shield.

Yet after the two men had fought for hours and night began to set in, they agreed it was time to stop and pledged to continue the fight the next morning. Moreover, their heroic code of honor dictated that they say farewell on friendly terms and even exchange gifts. Ajax handed Hector an expensive purple belt, and the Trojan gave Ajax a fine sword with a silver hilt.

Ajax's most striking display of honor occurred following Achilles's death. The other Greek leaders voted to give Achilles's armor to Odysseus, who was happy to receive that unexpected windfall. But in a moment of weakness, Ajax felt that he deserved to own the armor and for a while planned to resort to violence to get it. At the last moment, however, he came to his senses. Realizing how dishonorable he had been in coveting something that was not his, he killed himself by falling on his sword.

In these ways, Achilles, Odysseus, Hector, Ajax, and other mythical heroes of the Trojan War provided powerful examples for others to follow. To the classical Greeks, the *Iliad* was not merely an exciting, colorful adventure tale. It was also an essential manual for learning how to fight effectively and be brave, manly, and honorable.

```
回回回回回回回回回回回回回回回回回回回回回回回回回回
```

Heroes on Epic Quests and Journeys

O ne of the main themes of ancient Greek mythology is the heroic quest. Typically it involves a hero, usually male but on occasion female, who goes on a long or complicated journey to find something important. The object of the search varies, ranging from valuable or magical artifacts to the hero's homeland and, in one well-known case, a lost loved one.

During such an epic quest, the hero faces a number of challenges. They often include surviving the onslaught of storms, floods, or other natural forces; arguing or negotiating with and when necessary disobeying gods, goddesses, or other supernatural beings; fighting monsters and evil or troublesome humans; or solving mysteries by following various clues. Always the hero perseveres, no matter the odds, and almost always achieves his or her goal in the end.

Desiring to Right a Wrong

Nearly all of those standard aspects of the Greek mythological quest are found in the hero Jason's famous search for the fabulous Golden Fleece. That priceless hide of a one-of-a-kind flying ram was thought to have potent magical properties. Thus, the rulers of various kingdoms tried to get their hands on it.

Jason was a prince of Iolcos, a small kingdom in central Greece. The classical Greeks believed that his exploits took place during the Age of Heroes in the generation preceding the Trojan War. Of the

```
回回回回回回回回回回回回回回回回回回回回回回回回回回
```

The hero Jason takes possession of the Golden Fleece, a ram's hide thought to have magical powers, after killing the dragon guarding it. Jason's cousin, Pelias, sent him on this dangerous mission in hopes that Jason would be killed and he could continue to usurp Jason's rightful place as king of Iolcos.

many written works describing Jason's quest by those later Greeks, the most comprehensive was the *Argonautica* by the third-century BCE Greek poet Apollonius of Rhodes. The first-century CE Roman writer Valerius Flaccus also wrote a version of the same myth bearing the same title. Both authors used that title because it was common to call the story of the quest for the Golden Fleece the Argonautica. It referred to the fact that Jason and his men sailed in a ship named the *Argo* and were therefore known as the Argonauts.

The epic search for the Golden Fleece began shortly after Jason, then in his early twenties, found out about his birthright. He had been brought up in the countryside by his teacher, Chiron, and did not know that he was the son of Aeson, Iolcos's former king. After Chiron finally told Jason about his father, he also informed him that his cousin Pelias, the present king, had stolen the throne from Aeson.

Motivated to right that wrong—a trait all Greek heroes share—Jason journeyed to Iolcos and introduced himself to Pelias. As Aeson's son and thus the lawful king, the younger man demanded that Pelias hand over the throne. The greedy Pelias was desperate to hold on to power, but he also wanted to avoid fighting a civil war against Jason and the many Iolcons who would surely back him. Therefore, the king cunningly pretended to agree with Jason's claim to the throne. Pelias consented to abdicate his title as king as soon as Jason carried out a special mission designed to prove to the people that he was fit to be a strong ruler.

A Distant but Real Land

The task Pelias proposed was to capture the legendary Golden Fleece and bring it back to Iolcos. The priceless object was said to hang in a tree in the distant land of Colchis. Pelias, however, had ulterior motives. He expected that Jason would be killed during the long and dangerous voyage; thus, he would be rid of Jason and would be able to remain ruler of Iolcos.

Jason was confident he would get the fleece and immediately began preparations for the expedition. He found a master shipbuilder named Argus who constructed a magnificent vessel—the *Argo*. Also, for his crew Jason gathered together a remarkable band of heroes, true men of strength and action (*drasis* in Greek). Strongest of all was the mighty monster slayer Heracles. Other notable Argonauts included the skilled warrior Peleus; the

> **WORD ORIGINS**
>
> *drasis*
>
> In ancient Greece: action.
>
> In modern life: drastic, meaning typified by an extreme action.

The Argonauts and the Harpies

Of the numerous fascinating exploits described in the myth of the Argonautica, one of the more colorful occurred on the coast of the Bosphorus (one of the two narrow channels that separate the Aegean and Black Seas). There, the Argonauts came upon an old man named Phineus. Terribly starved looking, he told them he was in *agonia* ("agony") because of the Harpies, which were hideous flying female creatures with sharp claws. Every time he went to consume a meal, he explained, the monsters would swoop down and either take his food or cover it with their disgusting bodily fluids, rendering it unfit to eat.

Fortunately for Phineus, two of the *Argo's* crew, Zetes and Calais, were the sons of Boreas, the north wind, so they were able to fly. Taking advantage of that fact, Jason ordered his men to set a trap for the Harpies. They heaped mounds of delicious food in front of Phineus, hid, and waited for the filthy creatures to appear. When the Harpies swooped down to steal the food, Zetes and Calais intervened and chased them through the clouds. Finally cornering the beasts, the two Greeks would have slain them if not for the sudden appearance of Iris, goddess of the rainbow. The attractive sister of the horrible Harpies, she promised to keep them away from Phineus if the men would spare the creatures' lives. A deal was struck. The Harpies got to live and thereafter Phineus was able to eat his meals uninterrupted.

talented musician Orpheus; and Castor and Polydeuces, the twin sons of the god Zeus and a mortal woman. Soon the ship and crew were ready for the long and fateful voyage to faraway Colchis, said to lie on the little-known eastern shores of the Black Sea.

If one looks at a map today, the Black Sea appears to rest fairly close to Greece. But in the early years of Greece's classical era, that large waterway, especially its eastern portions, seemed both remote and mysterious to the Greeks. Nevertheless, they knew that the Black Sea and Colchis were both real destinations. They were drawn to stories, even ones featuring monsters and other fantastic elements, that were set in familiar locations because that gave such tales a feeling of authenticity. This was "the miracle of Greek mythology," the late renowned myth-teller Edith Hamilton writes. Those stories, she points out, take place in "a humanized world," where people are "freed from the paralyzing fear of an omnipotent unknown." The Greeks "disliked the irrational and had a love for facts," she adds, "no matter how wildly fantastic some of the stories are. Anyone who reads them with attention discovers that even the most nonsensical take place in a world which is essentially rational and matter-of-fact."[11]

Talos and His Boulders

Returning to Jason's story, the *Argo* sailed northward toward and finally into the Black Sea, and over the course of several months the crew experienced numerous adventures and dangers. At one point, for example, they barely made it through a deep channel bordered by the frightening Clashing Rocks, which constantly smashed together, crushing anything caught between them. The men also found a temple of the war god Ares. The structure was guarded by thousands of birds, which attacked the Argonauts, who managed to fight their way back to the ship.

Eventually the ships reached Colchis, where a cruel and shifty man named Aeetes was king. Jason asked him to hand over the Golden Fleece, but Aeetes refused. Lying through his teeth, the king said that he might consider it if Jason could yoke two monstrous fire-breathing bulls, use them to plow a field, and plant dragons' teeth there. Those seeds would swiftly grow into hundreds of armed warriors whom Jason must defeat. Only after accomplishing those feats would the chief Argonaut receive the Golden Fleece.

Aeetes felt certain that his unwanted guest would fail to complete the tasks demanded of him. The ruler therefore was shocked when

> ## WORD ORIGINS
>
> ### *agonia*
>
> In ancient Greece: agony.
>
> In modern life: agony, meaning severe pain; and agonistic, or related to conflict.

Jason succeeded, secretly aided by Aeetes's own daughter, the sorceress Medea, who had fallen in love with the young Greek at first sight. Wasting no time, Jason fought and killed a dragon that guarded the Golden Fleece. Then he took both that coveted prize and Medea to the *Argo* and sailed for Iolcos.

On the way home the Argonauts passed near the large Greek island of Crete. There, according to Apollonius, a giant bronze warrior named Talos stood guard and hurled huge boulders at the *Argo* and other vessels in an attempt to keep them from landing. The episode with Talos may well be based on a real and pivotal event from Greek history. A few miles north of Crete lies the tiny volcanic isle of Thera (modern Santorini). During the Bronze Age, unbeknownst to the later classical Greeks, the Theran volcano erupted with tremendous violence, sending enormous rocks flying outward for many miles.

Minoan and/or Mycenaean sailors who viewed the eruption from farther north would surely have told others that they had seen big rocks flying outward from the direction of Crete. It is unlikely that the seamen would have understood that those missiles came from a volcano. More logical to them was that someone or something had thrown them, and the most reasonable explanation was that the culprit was a giant. Thus, in succeeding generations storytellers added the tale of Talos and his boulders to the evolving myth of Jason and the Argonauts.

Odysseus's Adventures

After they returned to Greece, the Argonauts went their separate ways, and some continued on to other exploits. Heracles, for instance, completed the last four of his famous twelve labors after taking part in the Argonautica. Other Argonauts had sons who later fought in the great siege at Troy.

Another of Greek mythology's great heroic quests took place directly after that renowned conflict. Although the Greeks won, while they were sacking the city one of them committed an act of sacrilege, or disrespect for the gods, in a local temple. The irate sea god Poseidon meted out punishment for that offense by creating a huge storm that pounded hundreds of the Greek ships as they were on their way back to their homelands.

The contingent of Greeks that suffered the most from this catastrophe was the twelve-vessel fleet commanded by Odysseus, ruler of the island kingdom of Ithaca. Blown far off course, he and his men were forced to wander for years, encountering numerous strange lands and dangerous adventures. In one unpleasant episode, they tangled with the Lotus-Eaters, a race of beings whose food made people forget who they were. Other bizarre experiences along the way included a run-in with giant cannibals who ate many of Odysseus's crewmen; a witch who turned several of the Greeks into pigs; and death-defying clashes with a monstrous serpent and an enormous, ship-crushing whirlpool.

One of the scariest and probably the most famous of Odysseus's heroic exploits was his confrontation with a Cyclops—a one-eyed giant—named Polyphemus. "We arrived in the country of the Cyclopes," Odysseus said (according to Homer in the *Odyssey*). They were

The Cyclops Polyphemus roars in agony. The pole used by the Greeks to blind him still protrudes from his single eye, while Odysseus's ship escapes into the distance.

Myth-Tellers' Corner: Apuleius

The only surviving written source for the myth of Eros and Psyche is *The Golden Ass,* a Latin novel penned by the second-century CE Roman writer Apuleius. A native of one of Rome's North African provinces, he was born in about 125 CE. Not much is known about his life beyond the fact that he studied philosophy in Athens and was later accused of using magic to seduce a wealthy widow. Fortunately for him, a court cleared him of that charge.

The earlier Greek sources on which Apuleius based his version of the heroic Psyche's tale were lost in the centuries following his death. The episode with Psyche and Eros appears as a separate story told within the novel's main story. Apuleius initially titled the book *Metamorphoses,* meaning "physical changes." This was meant as a tribute to an earlier collection of myths of the same title by the first-century BCE Roman poet Ovid. Apuleius's version was about a young man who is transformed into a donkey and later back into a person. The novel permanently acquired the title *The Golden Ass* after the Latin Christian writer St. Augustine coined it in the early 400s CE.

"a brutal, uncultured people, who never bother to farm for their food, but instead trust in the aid of fate and the gods." Also, they "dwell in mountain caves, where each individual makes the laws for his own family and feels no concern for others of his kind."[12]

After Odysseus and some of his men found themselves trapped in Polyphemus's cave, that gruesome brute killed and ate six of the Greeks before Odysseus hatched an escape plan. One night the Cyclops got drunk and fell asleep. Odysseus then instructed the others to sharpen a wooden pole and heat the tip in the fire the creature had made, after which they drove that beam directly into Polyphemus's eye.

Awakening with a start, the giant "let out a horrible screech that bounced from one cave wall to the other." With the beast blinded, the Greeks were able to escape the cave and get back to their ship. Staggering after them, Polyphemus "broke off the top of a hill with his bare hands and threw it at us,"[13] Odysseus later recalled. The object struck the water and stirred up a tall wave, but the Greeks managed to get away.

Greece's Seafaring Tradition

Odysseus's fateful wanderings lasted ten years, during which he lost all his ships and men. Finally, he made it home to his wife and son in Ithaca, having sailed thousands of miles through both known and unknown seas and rivers. A constant theme in this long, exciting story, as well as in the myth of the Argonautica, was the Greeks' prowess as seafarers. Clearly the Bronze Age Minoans and Mycenaeans, from whose world so many of the myths came, had been expert sailors. Later, partly inspired by detailed descriptions of ships and sailors in those myths, the classical Greeks carried on that nautical tradition.

In fact, many Greeks were forced to become sailors because of the geographic conditions in which they lived. Greece's mainland has nearly two thousand miles (3,200 km) of coastline, and its hundreds of nearby islands add significantly more miles of seashores. This situation had two major outcomes that affected Greek life. First, Greek traders in spacious cargo vessels plied not only the Aegean and Mediterranean Seas but also the Black Sea, where they purchased huge amounts of wheat and other crops. Greek merchants also obtained all sorts of luxury goods from cities in Egypt, Syria, Italy, North Africa, Spain, and elsewhere. All that commerce made Athens, Corinth, and other large classical Greek states extremely prosperous.

The second important outcome of the maritime tradition the Greeks inherited from their myth-shrouded past was that several Greek states became leading naval powers and colonizers during the classical era. Athens, for example, mimicked the mythical Cretan king Minos, whose war fleets dominated and bullied all of the Aegean's coastal peoples. The classical Athenians constructed the largest fleet of warships in the Mediterranean basin during the 400s BCE. That allowed them to create an empire comprising more than a hundred widely dispersed coastal cities. Meanwhile, Rhodes, Corinth, Samos, and Miletus were only some of the classical Greek states that planted colonies along the Mediterranean and Black Sea coasts between 750 and 550 BCE.

A Connection with the Divine

Seafaring played no role, however, in a third well-known Greek myth about a gallant quest. In this case, the principal character was one of the few known female ancient mythical heroes. Her name was Psyche, a Greek word meaning "the mind" or "the soul." The daughter of a king and queen of a nameless, faraway city, she was so beautiful that people traveled from across the known world simply to gaze on her.

In fact, some people were so impressed by Psyche that they began to neglect their usual worship of Aphrodite, goddess of love and beauty. Instead, they started worshipping Psyche. When Aphrodite heard this, she became angry and called for her handsome son Eros to help her punish the young woman. His orders were to pretend to be the ugliest, most disgraceful man in the world and to make Psyche fall madly in love with him. That way her great good looks would be wasted and her life unhappy.

The problem was that Eros fell deeply in love with Psyche at his first sight of her. He tried to carry out his mother's dastardly plan by pretending to be an evil, repulsive being, but he could not bring himself to harm the young woman. Moreover, she detected that he was really a good person, fell in love with him, and eventually found a way to sneak a look at his true form.

When Eros realized that Psyche had discovered his real identity, he was worried about what his mother might do. In a sudden fit of indecision, he fled. Now realizing that she was in love with a god, and that he loved her as well, Psyche became determined to find him, even if it took the rest of her life. In a truly heroic effort, she searched and searched but was not able to locate him. Eventually the still angry

This nineteenth-century painting depicts Eros (later known as Cupid) approaching Psyche at the behest of his mother, Aphrodite, to carry out a revenge plot against the beautiful young woman. According to the myth, the plot fails when Eros instead falls in love with Psyche, eventually leading to a marriage between the two.

Aphrodite attained her revenge on Psyche by making her fall into a deep, permanent sleep. Only when Eros came to his senses, rescued the mortal woman he loved, and married her did the story finally achieve a happy ending.

All of the ancient written versions of this charming tale are lost but one—a section of the novel *The Golden Ass* by the Roman writer Apuleius. As a result, it is now more often called the myth of Cupid and Psyche since *Cupid* was the Latin version of *Eros*. However, the classical Greeks knew and enjoyed the story, as evidenced by the many paintings and sculptures they based on it, some as early as the fourth century BCE. To them, the power of the tale lay partly in the heroism of Psyche, who refused to give up her quest for the one she loved. She even braved a journey alone into the dark and scary underworld in hopes of finding him.

Also, the Greeks saw Psyche and Eros's myth as a perfect depiction of the way the world and society operated in the wondrous Age of Heroes. They believed that it was a time when the gods frequently interacted with mortals, including sometimes achieving *phila*, or "friendship," or even marriage with each other. In that respect, the Greeks were haunted by the story because it captured a piece of the human soul they felt was missing in their own time. Psyche, whose very name meant "the soul," reminded them of a glorious bygone era when at least some humans had had a chance to experience a close physical connection with the divine.

WORD ORIGINS

phila

In ancient Greece: friendship.

In modern life: Philadelphia, the "City of Brotherly Love," founded by the Quakers, or Society of Friends.

Chapter Three

Moving Tales of Heroic Lovers

The ancient Greeks had many myths about love and lovers. Quite often in those tales, the strong, loving bond between the two main characters was the central focus of the plot. In a few of those tales, however, a second theme was no less important than true love itself. That second premise was a noteworthy display of heroism by one of the lovers, in some cases including a willingness to risk all or even die so that the other lover might live.

Descent into the Depths

For many classical Greeks, the thought of a heroic lover immediately conjured up the image of Orpheus. In mythology, he was a talented poet who also composed astoundingly moving *melos*, or "music." Indeed, when he played his lyre (a small, handheld harp) and sang, nearby people and animals, along with trees, rocks, and other natural objects, were enthralled. Humans and even gods were moved to tears by the simplicity and beauty of his tunes. Also, when Orpheus served Jason as one of the Argonauts who searched for the Golden Fleece, the sounds that issued from that master musician's lyre made the *Argo* glide across the sea's surface faster than any other existing vessel.

One day while traveling through the countryside, spreading joy with his music, Orpheus met and instantly fell deeply in love with a lovely young woman named Eurydice. She loved him back and they married. The two were extremely happy together for a few short years until suddenly their lives turned upside down. Eurydice was bitten by a venomous snake, and despite the best efforts of healers in her village, she died. Her soul departed her body and Thanatos, the divine spirit of death, guided it down into the murky depths of the underworld.

Devastated by this terrible loss, Orpheus found that he could neither eat nor sleep. Unlike most people who lose a loved one, he became determined to do something extraordinary—to bring Eurydice back from the domain of death and into the world of the living. In an exhibition of unparalleled heroism, he risked his own life by descending downward into the dark depths of the kingdom of Hades, keeper of deceased human souls.

WORD ORIGINS

melos

In ancient Greece: music.

In modern life: melody, a recognizable tune heard in a piece of music.

One Crucial Condition

After searching for days, Orpheus found Hades's foreboding palace and confronted that deity and his queen, Persephone. Unafraid, the man raised his lyre and began to play and sing a special song he had prepared. It told how Eurydice was supremely good, an innocent whose life had been snatched from her in an untimely fashion. Through the song, the musician pleaded with Hades to allow the young woman to return to the land of the living. If she could not be released, Orpheus chanted, he would gladly give up his own life and remain in the underworld forever, just to be near her.

Orpheus's song was so haunting that Hades's cheerless heart melted, as did those of the demonic beings who had gathered around to hear the music. "For the first time," the Roman myth-teller Ovid writes, their cheeks "were wet with tears, for they were overcome by his singing." Moreover, "the king and queen of the underworld could not bear to refuse his pleas."[14] Hades agreed to allow Eurydice to leave his subterranean realm along with Orpheus. One crucial condition was that the man must walk ahead of her and could not glance back at her until they reached the outer sunlit world.

Orpheus followed that directive to the letter in the hours that followed. Although he dearly desired to gaze on his wife's smiling face

Orpheus is a main character in one of the Greek myths featuring themes of love. Said to play music so beautifully that it mesmerized people and animals alike, Orpheus used this talent to persuade Hades, king of the underworld, to release his beloved, Eurydice, from the god's dark realm.

once more, he stifled the temptation to do so. At the very last moment before reaching the surface, however, he was no longer able to control himself. In Ovid's words, "the lover looked behind him and straightaway Eurydice slipped back into the depths. Orpheus stretched out his arms, straining to clasp her, but the hapless man touched nothing but yielding air." Uttering "a last farewell which scarcely reached his ears, she fell back again into the same place from which she had come."[15]

Orpheus's Later Worshippers

The classical Greeks felt that this heartrending story taught some important moral and religious lessons. First, Hades had warned Orpheus not to look back. Yet the man had given in to temptation and done so. Thus, humans who chose to disobey direct orders issued by the gods were bound to pay a heavy price. Also, people should always try to

Myth-Tellers' Corner: Euripides

Born in about 485 BCE, Euripides was, along with Aeschylus and Sophocles, one of the three masters of fifth-century BCE Athenian tragedy. One of Euripides's hallmarks as a playwright was that he often emphasized themes and ideas that questioned traditional religious and social values. Another was that he frequently portrayed the problems and actions of socially marginal characters, such as slaves and women. As a result, modern experts view him as the first dramatist to depict human problems in a modern manner.

Some ancient sources claim that Euripides wrote eighty-eight or more plays, of which most dealt with mythological events and characters. Of his nineteen dramas that have survived complete, *Alcestis,* first presented in 438 BCE, is the oldest. Among the others are *Medea, The Suppliant Women, Electra,* and *Helen,* all of which address the exploits and dilemmas of strong women. Their solutions to their problems are often violent and controversial.

For instance, Antigone challenges her king's orders by burying her condemned brother's body and dies for it, Medea slays her own children to achieve revenge on her unfaithful husband, and Electra helps her brother kill their mother to punish her for murdering their father. Yet in all cases, Euripides manages to evoke at least some pity or even admiration for the mythical female lead. Indeed, the great Athenian scholar and thinker Aristotle said in his *Poetics* that Euripides was the most skilled of the tragic playwrights at arousing emotions like pity.

maintain self-control, particularly in life-and-death situations like the one Orpheus was in.

In addition, for the rest of his days Orpheus suffered intense, almost unbearable guilt for his mistake. That guilt actually became the basis for a religious sect that arose in the Greek lands during the classical era and remained on the fringes of Greek and later Greco-Roman society for many centuries to come. Called Orphism, after Orpheus, it was based on some secret writings that he supposedly had composed and passed on to later generations. These texts claimed that humans everywhere were haunted by collective guilt for an original sin. That crime was the murder of an obscure god named Dionysus Zagreus, said to have existed sometime in the dim past.

To cleanse oneself of this inborn offense, a worshipper had to reincarnate, or be reborn in a new body, three times in a row. If that person led a moral, sinless life each time, he or she was allowed to enter the Isles of the Blessed, a part of the underworld where heroes' souls purportedly spent eternity. Therefore, like a later ancient religion—Christianity—Orphism held out the promise of ultimate happiness in an afterlife in exchange for avoiding sin.

Penthesilea and Achilles

In Orpheus's tale, only one of the lovers proved to be a hero, although a tragic one in the end. In contrast, in another Greek myth about love, both main characters were heroes. In fact, each had been widely recognized as such well before they met. Another unusual, and somewhat dark, aspect of the myth is that only one of the figures in question actually fell in love because the other was already dead.

The female hero in the tale was Penthesilea, a queen of the Amazons, the famous tribe of warrior women who were said to dwell somewhere in the wild, little-known lands lying far north of Greece. During the Trojan War, Troy's king, Priam, contacted the Amazons. He said he needed their aid to fight the Greeks who were besieging his city. Penthesilea, who disliked all Greeks, eagerly responded by marching a small army of her female soldiers to Troy.

Entering a battle that was then raging in the wide plain in front of the city, Penthesilea killed three skilled Greek warriors in a row. In fact, she appeared to be so fierce and capable that most Greeks feared to challenge her. One of their number was *not* afraid of her, however. Achilles, widely viewed as the greatest of the Greek fighters, rushed right at Penthesilea. They sparred for several minutes as both Greeks and Trojans stopped to watch. Although the muscular and well-trained Amazon was indeed a formidable warrior, she was no match for her opponent. Achilles finally found an opening and buried the tip of his spear into her chest, piercing her heart.

But at that moment, something extremely unusual occurred. As Penthesilea's body began to sag toward the ground, Achilles suddenly looked at her with fresh eyes and instantly fell in love with her. Reaching out, he caught her limp corpse in his arms and gently laid her down in the blood-soaked dirt. As one ancient writer tells it, "She was made a wonder of beauty even in her death." Meanwhile, Achilles's "heart was wrung with love's remorse to have slain a thing so sweet." He now saw that "she was flawless, a very daughter of the gods, divinely tall and most divinely fair."[16] His love for the woman he had killed remained strong right up until he himself met death on that plain later in the war.

The classical Greeks viewed this myth about Achilles's sudden love for Penthesilea as quite out of the ordinary. Put simply, most Greeks could not imagine women in their society becoming soldiers. War and expertise in weapons were strictly the province of men, whereas women were expected to spend most of their time in the home doing the cooking and cleaning and raising the children. The idea that such female warriors, including Penthesilea, had once actually existed seemed fascinating and compelling for its novelty.

The Greeks also liked Penthesilea's story because it helped to flesh out one of their favorite characters—Achilles. In most myths he was a sober, no-nonsense killing machine with no indication of an emotional, sensitive side. His love for Penthesilea gave him that added dimension. As Madeline Miller, author of *Song of Achilles*, points out, "Achilles sees in her a sort of kindred spirit, another fierce and flashing youth, proud and driven towards honor."[17]

WORD ORIGINS

aristocrat

In modern life: a member of a social class viewed as noble or better than average folk.

In ancient Greece: *aristos*, meaning best.

Antigone's Sad Tale

Another heroic Greek myth about love dealt not with male-female romantic ties but rather with the close familial feelings between a sister and her brother. In this case, the sister was Antigone, daughter of Oedipus, ruler of the ancient kingdom of Thebes. As leading aristocrats, or nobles, Antigone and her siblings—her sister, Ismene, and her two brothers, Polynices and Eteocles—became entangled in a major crisis after Oedipus was forced to give up his throne. (It had recently been revealed that he had inadvertently slain the former king, his father.)

The emergency arose when Polynices and Eteocles heatedly argued about which of them should replace their father as king. Eventually they agreed that Eteocles would rule for a year while Polynices went into exile. Then, Polynices would rule the following year while

After Oedipus, king of Thebes, was forced to give up his throne, his sons Polynices and Eteocles argued about which of them would take his place. Eventually, they agreed to decide the question in single combat. This nineteenth-century painting depicts the brutal fight, witnessed by Jocasta, the mother of the two, and their sister Antigone.

Greek Women and Funerals

In Antigone's famous myth, her extreme concern to make sure that her brother received a proper burial reflected the same sort of concern felt by the members of classical Greek society. Also mirroring the myth was the fact that Antigone was a woman, and most of the preparation of dead bodies in classical Greece was done by women. The prevailing belief was that a dead person's soul could not get into the afterlife in the underworld unless the body first underwent certain set rituals. Usually, the family women were in charge of most of these rites. If the body was to be cremated, they prepared it and then collected the bones and ashes afterward and placed them in a special pottery urn. The women also made sure that the grave or tomb was supplied with libations—liquids such as wine or honey that were traditionally offered to the gods during a funeral. Importantly, the women led the inevitable displays of mourning. These were frequently loud and at times even forceful and bloody, as some women tore out clumps of their hair and/or dug their fingernails into their cheeks, leaving big scars. Most Greek women were second-class citizens who were expected to do what their fathers and husbands ordered. But they were given a largely free hand in carrying out funerals for the family dead. That is why the Greeks saw Antigone's concerns for her brother's proper burial in her myth as quite realistic and moving.

Eteocles left the city, and so forth. The problem was that after he ascended the throne, Eteocles decided to break the deal and reign permanently.

Naturally furious over this betrayal, Polynices raised an army and besieged Thebes, intent on driving his brother from the throne. After much strife, both sides agreed the brothers would engage in single combat and the winner would be king. In an outcome no one expected, however, the two young men slew each other. "Thebes is saved," a messenger states in the Athenian playwright Aeschylus's tragedy *Seven Against Thebes*. "But her two brother kings are fallen; the earth has drunk their blood, shed by each other's hands."[18]

Because Polynices had been attacking the city, the new king, Creon (the brothers' uncle), forbade him a proper burial. But Antigone, like a majority of Greeks, saw this order as barbaric, for without a decent burial her brother's soul would be doomed to wander aimlessly for eternity. Thus, out of love for Polynices, she defied the order and buried him. As a result of this bold, heroic act, Creon condemned Antigone to death and she was executed.

The classical Greeks paid close attention to mythical descriptions of social rituals surrounding death and burial. Indeed, those mythical depictions, along with the customs handed down by parents and grandparents, were the two main sources of such rituals. Antigone buried her brother's body, and that practice still was used sometimes in classical times. However, most people in the centuries following the Dark Age cremated their dead.

Whether a corpse was burned or buried, proper burial was viewed, as in Antigone's tale, as essential by the vast majority of Greeks. Typically, the family women prepared a body by washing it and dressing it in white garments. Usually the corpse lay in the house for a day or two so that relatives and friends could view it. Then they transported the body, now lying in a wooden or stone coffin, to the gravesite, which was located outside the city walls.

An *epitaphios*, or "funeral speech," was given at the gravesite, after which the body either was buried or burned. In the case of cremation, the ashes were placed in an urn and buried. Lastly, the mourners yelled out the dead person's name three times and departed. Failing to accord the deceased these basic rituals was considered disrespectful, even uncivilized.

Alcestis's Heroic Love

Death was also the main theme of one of the most moving of all the Greek myths that combined the concepts of love and heroism—the tale of brave Alcestis and her husband, Admetus. King of Pherae, in northern Greece, Admetus fell in love with and married Alcestis, a princess of a nearby city. The two were extremely happy together until Admetus learned from the god Apollo that he was fated to die in the near future. Because Apollo admired the good and generous Admetus, he granted him a special privilege. He could avoid his coming date with death, the deity explained, if he could locate another person who would freely choose to die in his place.

Admetus painstakingly searched but was unable to find a single individual who was willing to face death for him. The king was about to give up when his queen, Alcestis, heroically stepped forward and committed herself to giving up her life for him. It was not just that she was concerned that his death would leave the city *anarkhos*, meaning "without a ruler." She also loved him with all her heart and could not bear to think of his dying.

Thus, a few days later, while all the kingdom's inhabitants went into mourning for her, Alcestis quietly awaited the arrival of Thanatos, the god of death. He would lead her away, at which point her life would be over. However, not long before that morbid deity appeared, the renowned strongman Heracles reached the palace, learned what was happening, and planned to ambush Thanatos.

The wrestling match that ensued between those two powerful figures rocked the building for at least an hour. Finally, the god realized that no matter how hard he tried, he could not defeat Heracles and take custody of Alcestis. Thus, the thoroughly embarrassed Thanatos chose to silently slink away. A while later the victorious Heracles delivered the thankful queen to her husband, and everyone in the kingdom rejoiced.

WORD ORIGINS

anarkhos

In ancient Greece: lacking a ruler to provide social order.

In modern life: anarchy, a state of social disorder and chaos.

Alcestis, queen of Pherae, bravely chose to die so that the life of her husband, the king Admetus, would be spared. The hero Heracles, however, fought to keep her out of the clutches of Thanatos, god of death. Here, Heracles returns the rescued queen to her husband.

"A Deed of Supreme Excellence"

The classical Greeks were closely familiar with Alcestis's myth, especially after the Athenian playwright Euripides produced his version of it in 438 BCE. Playgoers found the story moving, in part because of the heroism that both Alcestis and Heracles displayed. Most Greeks also viewed Alcestis's deep love for her husband as touching. Unfortunately for many Greek couples, however, they were never able to experience that sort of romantic attraction and saw it largely as an ideal that was admirable but not very realistic.

This is because most marriages in classical Greece were arranged by fathers or other male family members. In fact, it was not unusual for a bride and a groom to know each other only casually, or even not at all, before they were married. Romantic love, which today is widely viewed as a major requirement of marriage, did exist in Greece. But thanks to the custom of arranging marriages, it was rare.

Thus, the Greeks viewed Alcestis's heroic act of love as something not commonly seen in their society. Nevertheless, they did hold her sacrifice in high regard. As the famous fourth-century BCE Athenian thinker Plato puts it in his *Symposium*, "She alone was willing to die for her husband." Plato adds that the gods greatly valued "loyalty and courage in love." In the end, even though female heroes of such stature were rare, "she was thought by men and gods alike to have performed a deed of supreme excellence."[19]

Chapter Four

Six Courageous Monster Slayers

*S*peaking about the typical Greek mythical hero, the late noted classical scholar Michael Grant said that he "must use his superior qualities at all times to excel and win applause, for that is the reward and demonstration of his manhood."[20] On the same topic, the late Joseph Campbell, a widely popular expert on world mythologies, wrote that the hero "ventures forth from the world of the common day into a region of supernatural wonder. Fabulous forces are there encountered and a decisive victory is won."[21]

The heroes of the Greek myths accomplished many and diverse feats. But when it came to demonstrating their manhood, dealing with the supernatural, and attaining decisive victories, one kind of heroic accomplishment surpassed all others—hunting down and slaying monsters. Those creatures were almost always gigantic. They were also hideous, vicious, and frightening; and they threatened the safety of villages, cities, or entire kingdoms or peoples. Nothing could stop them except for the valor, strength, and cleverness of a hero, sometimes with the aid of one or more gods.

The classical Greeks adored such tales. For them, listening to someone recite the story of how a hero from the dim past overcame a monster

> ## WORD ORIGINS
>
> ### gigantic
>
> In modern life: extremely large.
>
> In ancient Greece: *gigas*, meaning huge.

was the equivalent of people today going to the movies, watching favorite television shows, or playing video games. In large degree, it was a form of entertainment, although the hero-and-monster myths also possessed other qualities, such as teaching moral lessons and providing brief glimpses of what was thought to be Greece's early history.

Theseus in the Labyrinth

For example, the Greeks were sure that one of their best-known and favorite hero-and-monster myths—Theseus and the Minotaur—was largely historical. Moreover, based in part on that old tale, the classical Athenians looked upon Theseus as their national hero. During the Age of Heroes, the story went, he was the son of Athens's aged, kind, and just king Aegeus.

In his childhood, however, Theseus was raised elsewhere in Greece and did not know he was an Athenian prince. When as a young man he found out, he traveled to Athens and introduced himself to Aegeus, who happily welcomed him. The king also told his son about a serious dilemma the city then faced. Minos, the ruler of the large, rich, and powerful island of Crete, had for some time been bullying the militarily weaker Athens. Every few years Aegeus was forced to send fourteen young people—seven boys and seven girls—to Crete or else Minos would destroy Athens.

On arriving in Crete, Aegeus told Theseus, Minos threw the hostages into a massive, mazelike underground prison called the Labyrinth. Dwelling within those subterranean chambers was a gruesome, ferocious monster called the Minotaur. Half bull and half human, the creature devoured the Athenian hostages one by one.

Horrified by this state of affairs, Theseus became determined to put a stop to it. When the king sent the next group of hostages to Crete, the prince said, he would be among them and would make it his mission to destroy the menacing bull-man. "Theseus urged his father to take heart," writes his ancient Greek biographer Plutarch, "and boasted that he would overcome the Minotaur."[22]

Theseus got his chance the next time a Cretan ship arrived to pick up Athenian hostages. Leaving as one of them, when he got to Minos's capital he broke free and made his way into the extensive underground maze beneath the palace. Glancing around in the dim light emitted by

Classical Athenians considered the mythological character Theseus as their national hero. Pictured here is a scene from one of the best known tales about him, in which he slays the Minotaur, a dreadful beast half human and half bull to whom Athenian youths were sacrificed.

his torch, he saw the skulls and other bones of former Athenians who had met a grisly fate in that awful place.

Suddenly the man heard heavy breathing coming from up ahead. Raising his torch, he made out the enormous bulk of the monster, which snorted at him and strode forward expecting to claim its next victim. But Theseus was ready. Producing a rope lasso he had hidden in his cloak, he leapt into the air, tossed the torch into the creature's eyes to throw it off balance, and looped the lasso over its head. As the surprised Minotaur staggered to one side, the young man maneuvered behind its head and began choking it. The terrified bull-man rolled around in the dirt, trying its best to dislodge its attacker, but to no avail. Soon it was dead, and Theseus returned to Athens in triumph.

A Raid on the Capital?

To the classical Greeks, particularly the Athenians, Theseus's triumph over the Minotaur was not an isolated event. Instead, slaying the beast was part of a larger historical event—an Athenian attack on Minos's capital, an expedition intended to break Crete's political and likely military dominance over early Athens. The classical Athenians therefore interpreted Theseus's myth as a sort of chronicle of Athenian international relations during the Age of Heroes.

Myth-Tellers' Corner: Plutarch

Born in about 46 CE, Plutarch was a Greek-born biographer and moralist who became active in government affairs in his native city of Chaeronea (located several miles north of Athens). He also worked with some of the priests at Apollo's famous temple at Delphi and became a Roman citizen and lived for a while in Rome. He is best known for two enormous literary works. The first is his *Parallel Lives,* which consists of fifty detailed biographies of Greek and Roman rulers, military generals, and other well-known figures. The second is the *Moralia,* or *Moral Essays,* a collection of fascinating narratives on moral, ethical, political, literary, philosophic, scientific, and other issues.

Plutarch's works are valuable not only for the specific information they contain about his world but also because the sources he employed included numerous ancient historical and literary works that have not survived. Also, he provided a great deal of material about Greek mythology. For example, his biography of the Athenian national hero Theseus is by far the most comprehensive surviving ancient source on that character. He also wrote a lengthy biography of Romulus, the founder of Rome, which contains a wealth of detail about the myths associated with that pivotal event. In addition, most of Plutarch's essays make reference to various other myths, both well known and obscure.

Indeed, they envisioned that at a distance a fleet of Athenian war-ships, disguised as merchant vessels, followed the Cretan ship carrying the hostages. Then, sometime after Theseus landed in Crete, he signaled those ships to land and begin the assault. Another section of Plutarch's account states that shortly before Theseus set out with the hostages for Crete, King Minos was killed in a sea battle hundreds of miles away. Thus, the dead ruler's son, Deucalion, ascended Crete's throne and prepared to accept the doomed Athenian youths. "The Cretans had no warning of Theseus's movements," Plutarch continues,

> and supposed that the oncoming fleet [of Athenian vessels] was friendly, so that Theseus was able to seize the harbor, disembark his men, and reach [the capital] before his arrival was discovered. There he fought a battle at the gates of the [palace] and killed Deucalion and his bodyguard. As Ariadne [Minos's daughter] now succeeded to the throne, he made a truce with her, recovered the young Athenians, and concluded a pact of friendship between the Athenians and the Cretans, who swore that they would never in the future begin a war with Athens.[23]

Thus, the classical Greeks envisioned the slaying of the Minotaur as part of the story of how Theseus defeated the overbearing Cretans and put early Athens on the map as an Aegean military power. Furthermore, there may actually be something to that vision. The Minotaur itself was obviously not real. However, a number of modern experts think that the mythical Theseus himself may be based on a real Bronze Age Athenian military general who successfully raided the Cretan, more properly Minoan, capital of Knossos.

Heroes with Their Hands Full

Theseus was only one of many mythical Greek heroes who made their names killing monsters. Another was Perseus, said to be the son of a mortal mother and a divine father—Zeus, leader of the Greek gods. The young man took on the formidable task of finding and killing a hideous monster named Medusa. She was so repulsive that when people and animals looked directly at her, they turned to stone.

At first, Perseus had no idea where to look for Medusa. But his quest soon attracted the attention of two gods—the messenger-deity Hermes and Athena, goddess of war and wisdom. Hermes showed the young hero where the monster lived—a remote island near the edge of the known world. Then Athena visited Perseus and showed him how to avoid Medusa's murderous gaze and keep from turning to stone. The solution, she explained, was a shield of polished bronze, which she handed to him. If he looked only at the beast's reflection in the shield's surface, its normally deadly gaze would be harmless, Athena said. Perseus also benefitted from two gifts from some nature goddesses known as nymphs. They gave him a pair of winged sandals that allowed him to fly and a special cap that made its wearer invisible.

Armed with these formidable tools, the young man flew to the island, found Medusa, and wasted no time in attacking her. She could sense that danger was near, but thanks to the man's cap of invisibility, she could not see him. So being careful to view her only by reflection, Perseus was able to swing his sword and sever her monstrous head from her repulsive body.

Although Perseus had removed a major threat from his world, he and his fellow mythical heroes had their hands full, as a great many monsters menaced that world of the dim past. Particularly common was one type—the dragon, a huge *sauros*, or "lizard," often with wings and the ability to spit out deadly bursts of fire. Three of the most famous and destructive Greek dragons wreaked havoc in Thebes, located in the south-central Greek mainland; Lycia, a Greek cultural area in what is now southern Turkey; and the legendary land of Colchis, located on the Black Sea's eastern shore.

The hero who slew the Theban dragon, Cadmus, was also the founder of Thebes. When he tried to get water for the city's initial inhabitants, he discovered that the only viable stream was guarded by a dragon that killed and ate every traveler who passed through the area.

WORD ORIGINS

sauros

In ancient Greece: a lizard or other reptile.

In modern life: dinosaur, one of a number of extinct, reptile-like land creatures.

Cadmus, the founder of Thebes, made the region safe by slaying a dragon that guarded the water supply and ate any traveler who ventured near. Dragons were a common type of monster that inhabited the world depicted in Greek mythology.

Bold and a skilled warrior, Cadmus slaughtered the fearsome creature, thereby making the region safe. Meanwhile, a handsome young hero named Bellerophon destroyed the Lycian dragon, known as the Chimera. Likewise, Jason, famous for finding the Golden Fleece (the skin of a magical ram), eliminated the Colchian dragon.

Cadmus and the Theban Dragon

One of the more prominent Greek mythological heroes, Cadmus, was a native of Tyre, a city in Phoenicia, an ancient region located along the coasts of what are now Israel and Lebanon. His father ordered him to journey to Greece to find Cadmus's sister, Europa, whom the Greek god Zeus had taken to that faraway land. Once in Greece, Cadmus went to the famous oracle at Delphi and asked where Europa might be. The answer he received was that he no longer needed to search for his sister. Rather, he should see to his own needs and look for a cow. Cadmus should follow that animal through the countryside until it eventually lay down to rest, and on that spot he should found a new city. Just as prophesied, Cadmus soon saw the cow. He followed it, as instructed, toward the east, and when it finally sat down near a fertile plain, the young man established the new city, which became known as Thebes. Needing pure water for the town's residents, Cadmus took some men and went to a nearby stream. There, they found the stream guarded by a monstrous dragon. The beast swiftly slaughtered the other men before Cadmus drew his sword and leapt through the air at it. Over and over, he jabbed the weapon into the dragon's neck until the beast fell to the ground with a thud. This courageous act, which made a great city possible, was celebrated many centuries later by the classical Greeks.

"Slaying Fear Itself"

To the classical Greeks, their many myths about heroes who courageously fought and killed monsters were more than simply entertaining tales to tell around the family hearth. These stories also had an indirect religious connection. This was because at the time it was well known that killing monsters had started not with human heroes but rather with some of the major gods the Greeks worshipped.

The first and most important of those deities was Apollo, the wise god of prophecy, or foreseeing future events. He was also widely known as a deity of medicine, music, poetry, and archery as well as dragon slaying. That last area of expertise was based on a well-known feat in which he destroyed a monster in order to take possession of his famous temple at Delphi in central Greece. As researcher John Mancini puts it, "A spring nearby the location of the temple was guarded by the large Python, or she-dragon, which Apollo slew upon arrival." After that heroic act, "the traditional *omphalos* (a rounded stone artifact and early focal point of the temple) came to feature a carved snake wrapped around it. This marked it as a symbol of Apollo, the dragon-slayer, god of wisdom and healing."[24]

The temple at Delphi was known and respected throughout Greece and nearby lands throughout the classical period, as religious pilgrims journeyed there to ask the oracle, or local priestess, questions about their lives. The general view was that if Apollo had not killed the reptilian Python, that crucial aspect of Greek religion would never have come to pass. By emulating Apollo's monster slaying, therefore, Theseus, Perseus, Jason, and other human heroes were also seen as making civilized life in Greece possible.

In fact, the concept of civilization arising out of barbarism lay at the heart of why the Greeks were so fascinated by myths in which both heroes and gods slew such frightening creatures. "We can never be certain," Mancini writes, but the heroic act of ridding the countryside of monsters "could be seen as a symbolic act of taming the wild, the natural, the demonic." Primitive, seemingly unstoppable beasts that threatened humanity's very survival "embodied all the natural forces the ancients would have feared. Slaying them, meant slaying fear itself."[25]

The Mighty Heracles

One Greek mythical hero was widely renowned for eliminating fear and evil from the world more frequently and in more spectacular fashion than any other. The Greeks called him Heracles, but the Romans later tweaked it to Hercules, the name he is best known by today. He possessed not only tremendous physical strength but also humility, as he was willing to admit when he was wrong. Heracles had two glaring flaws: a bad temper and mediocre intelligence. Yet he managed to make up for these flaws to a great extent thanks to his big heart and readiness to apologize for his mistakes. In Edith Hamilton's words, his "thinking was limited to devising a way to kill a monster which was threatening to kill him. Nevertheless, he had true greatness. Not because he had complete courage based on overwhelming strength, which is a matter of course, but because, by his sorrow for wrongdoing and his willingness to do anything to expiate [make amends for] it, he showed greatness of soul."[26]

The mighty Heracles, as people often called him, performed all sorts of memorable feats. They included cleaning the world's filthiest horse stables; retrieving valuable objects from remote, dangerous regions; and leading the soldiers of his home city of Thebes against an army of invaders. But he was *most* famous for fighting and slaying either gruesome monsters or ordinary animals that were unusually large, fierce, and on a lethal rampage.

The first example of Heracles's monster killing took place when he was a mere toddler. He was the product of an affair between his mortal mother and the leader of the gods, Zeus. Wracked with jealousy, Zeus's divine wife, Hera, wanted to punish her husband, so she sent a pair of giant snakes into the nursery in Thebes to eat the new baby. Unafraid, the infant simply grasped one serpent in each hand and strangled the life out of them.

It was now clear to everyone involved with young Heracles, including Hera, that he possessed superhuman strength, almost certainly because he was Zeus's son. The next major test of that power came when the the boy was in his teens. Not far from Thebes, on Mt. Cithaeron, an enormous lion began eating entire herds of sheep belonging to local farmers. Heracles not only wrestled and slew the beast but also skinned it and thereafter wore its hide over his tunic.

A few years later Heracles visited Delphi and sought guidance from the famous oracle of Apollo. The priestess advised the young strongman to journey southward to the Peloponnesus and meet with one of its local kings, Eurystheus. That ruler said he had a series of seemingly impossible tasks that needed doing and challenged the muscular visitor to attempt them.

Among those so-called twelve labors that Heracles eventually completed, no less than seven involved killing or capturing monsters or out-of-control animals. First, he strangled the Nemean Lion, a massive cat that was invulnerable to wounds by ordinary weapons. After that, the young man fought and slew the Hydra, a nine-headed dragon that dwelled in a dismal swamp; a monstrous boar running

Of the twelve challenges, or labors, that the hero Heracles accepted from Peloponnesian king Eurystheus, seven involved slaying a monster of some sort. One of these was the Hydra, a hideous nine-headed swamp-dwelling creature.

amok in the eastern Peloponnesus; a flock of giant birds that killed people using sharp metal blades embedded in their feathers; and a herd of human-eating horses plaguing the far northern Greek region of Thrace. Heracles also captured and later released a savage bull that the sea god Poseidon had given to Crete's King Minos, and he did the same with Cerberus, the huge and vicious three-headed dog that guarded the entrance to the underworld. Considering these amazing feats, it is no wonder that, of the many mythical monster-slaying heroes the classical Greeks revered, Heracles was far and away the most beloved and unforgettable.

Chapter Five

Greek Heroes in Later Western Culture

The heroic myths that developed in the centuries preceding the rise of the classical Greeks were closely related to ancient Greek religion. After all, the gods that the Greeks revered frequently interacted with the heroes in those stories. Moreover, a number of other myths purported to show how those deities preferred to be worshipped. In addition, in the early years of the classical period, most people assumed that the feats the heroes and gods had long ago performed were real events.

In the centuries that followed, however, Greek and Roman views of the traditional myths changed. At first, the relatively few highly educated folk, and later most ordinary people as well, came to believe that those stories were mainly just entertaining folktales. Furthermore, when Christianity began replacing traditional Greco-Roman religion during the 200s and 300s CE, the connection between the myths and religion steadily dissipated.

Even so, most of those stories survived. As the centuries passed, they were absorbed into the arts, literature, music, and other cultural aspects of the European-based kingdoms and nations that arose upon the old Greco-Roman world's decaying ruins. Today the heroes populating classical mythology remain vividly alive. As in the past, each new generation of poets, playwrights, novelists, composers, and other creative individuals continues to exploit the heroes and their memorable mythical achievements.

The World in a Whole New Light

Thus, the Greek heroic myths underwent a long transformation from what the early Greeks saw as factual narratives to what people today cherish as entertaining cultural folklore. In retrospect, the first time that anyone questioned the validity of those stories was sometime during the 500s BCE. Several of the first Greek philosophers, who were also the world's first scientists, started to view the universe, which they called the *kosmos*, in a whole new light. They suspected that the world had been shaped by natural forces rather than by divine beings. If that was true, then the *palaeos*, or very old, stories of the gods creating the universe had likely been made up; and if so, other myths, including the ones about Heracles, Odysseus, and other legendary heroes, might also be mere folktales.

For a while only the handful of existing scholars harbored such suspicions about the ancient myths. This is not surprising considering that the vast majority of Greeks before the early 400s BCE could neither read nor write and lacked formal educations. But as the classical era continued to unfold, more and more Greeks became educated; as a result, some started to question certain age-old beliefs. In the late 400s BCE, for example, men called Sophists appeared on the scene. Teachers who, for a price, offered people instruction in reading, mathematics, and other practical subjects, they also urged their students to question the status quo. This caused an increasing number of people to question the authenticity, or reality, of the gods and mythical heroes. Such changing attitudes led Plato, the famous Athenian thinker of the following century, to eliminate Homer's accounts of Achilles, Hector, and other heroes of the Trojan War from his proposed ideal educational curriculum.

This sort of thinking about mythology gained strength during the third century BCE. Greek scholars like Callimachus and Euhemerus of Messene specialized in analyzing the old myths and offering logical explanations for their origins. Euhemerus became widely known for

Young men study at the feet of teachers in ancient Athens. As education became more widespread in Greece, people began to question whether myths described actual events. Many scholars believed that mythical heroes had been real people whose achievements had been exaggerated over the centuries.

his theory that the major Greek gods, along with celebrated heroes like Theseus and Perseus, had actually been very ancient human rulers and military heroes. Over many centuries, he claimed, their stories had undergone gross exaggeration, in the process endowing those characters with superhuman or magical powers.

The Heroes Survive in Literature

Still another blow to the Greek myths, including those about military, romantic, and monster-slaying heroes, came when Christianity rose to prominence as the Roman Empire's chief religious faith in the late 300s CE. Most Christians rejected the validity of the old myths outright. During the century or more that followed, meanwhile, many Romans and Greeks remained pagans (non-Christians) and continued worshipping the old gods in private. Even they no longer thought that the events described in the myths had actually happened. Yet they

Myth-Tellers' Corner: Edith Hamilton

Born in Dresden, Germany, in 1867, Edith Hamilton grew up in Fort Wayne, Indiana, and later became one of the greatest classical scholars of the twentieth century. She also had the distinction of writing the most famous book about Greek mythology published in modern times—*Mythology: Timeless Tales of Gods and Heroes.* The first edition appeared in 1940, and new editions have been printed nearly every year right up to the present, as colleges and universities around the world continue to use it as primary reading for classes on mythology, ancient Greece, and Western civilization.

Hamilton received her master's degree in classics in 1894 from prestigious Bryn Mawr College and went on to successful twin careers as a teacher and writer. In addition to her renowned book of myths, she also published two other seminal volumes on the roots of Western civilization—*The Greek Way* and *The Roman Way,* both of which are also still used in schools.

Hamilton died in 1963. In the foreword to her mythology book, she wrote, "My hope is that those who do not know the classics will gain in this way not only a knowledge of the myths, but some little idea of what the writers were like who told them." She had no notion then that people would one day view her as equal in stature to those great ancient myth-tellers.

Edith Hamilton, *Mythology: Timeless Tales of Gods and Heroes.* New York: Grand Central, 2011, p. 5.

proudly held on to those tales as treasured remnants of their cultural past.

Thus, the exciting tales of Achilles, Orpheus, Theseus, Jason, and the other Greek heroes remained part of Western culture throughout the medieval period (ca. 500–1600) and on into the early modern era that followed. Those myths never lost their power to entertain. So it is not surprising that early modern poets, playwrights, and other writers frequently made reference to the Greek heroes. The famous sixteenth-century English playwright William Shakespeare, for instance, mentioned the Greek heroes hundreds of times in his works. The renowned strongman Heracles (whom he called Hercules) is alluded to no less than forty-eight times in eighteen of Shakespeare's plays. According to noted literary scholar Charlotte Coffin, those references to Hercules "span Shakespeare's entire career, [and] comparisons help define more than 20 male characters, from Petruccio [in *The Taming of the Shrew*] to Arcite [in *Two Noble Kinsmen*]. But in most cases, Hercules is evoked in a general way, as the *exemplum* [perfect model] of the hero."[27]

Western literary references to the Greek mythical heroes continued in the centuries following Shakespeare's time and were particularly abundant during the twentieth century and the early years of the twenty-first. Two outstanding examples in the twentieth century were English writer Robert Graves's 1944 novel *The Golden Fleece*, also known as *Hercules, My Shipmate* and Irishman James Joyce's acclaimed 1922 novel *Ulysses*. The latter looks at the shortcomings of modern society by tracing the journeys of Leopold Bloom, a character who mirrors the hero Odysseus (Ulysses to the Romans) in Homer's *Odyssey*. A few of the numerous memorable early twenty-first-century novels about the Greek mythical heroes include Mike Chapman's *Achilles* (2004), Glyn Iliffe's *The Gates of Troy* (2009), and Katherine Beutner's *Alcestis* (2010).

WORD ORIGINS

palaeos

In ancient Greece: very old.

In modern life:
paleontology, the study of
very ancient life-forms.

Great Artists Tackle the Heroes

In the same way that they inspired playwrights, poets, and novelists, the Greek myths about heroes served as compelling material for painters, sculptors, and other artists. Of the many paintings of famous heroes by the early great masters, one of the most famous is the 1610 work

Perseus and Andromeda by Italy's Morazzone (Pier Francesco Mazzucchelli). It shows the sword-wielding hero attacking a sea monster that threatens to kill and eat Andromeda, a beautiful princess. Another painter, the Flemish master Peter Paul Rubens, turned out a canvas with the same subject and title in 1622. Moreover, the noted English artist Frederick "Lord" Leighton did the same in 1891.

Perseus was only one of the Greek heroes captured forever in oil paint on canvas. Twelve years before he painted Medusa's killer, Leighton had tackled the female hero Psyche in his *Bath of Psyche* (presently on display at London's Tate Gallery). Also, Italian artist Pellegrino Tibaldi's renowned 1550 canvas, *The Blinding of Polyphemus,* was only one of many major paintings showing the hero Odysseus's confrontation with the giant Cyclops.

Many sculptors were also inspired by Perseus's myths, but to date none of their works have matched the popularity of the great Italian master Benvenuto Cellini's *Perseus with the Head of Medusa.* Even today this magnificent bronze work, completed in 1554, remains a major tourist attraction in Florence, Italy. The statue, towering 18 feet (5.5 m) high, shows the renowned mythical monster slayer triumphantly standing and holding his sword in his right hand and the head of the dead monster in his left.

Still another artist who was celebrated for his depictions of Greek mythical heroes was Germany's Albrecht Dürer. His highly inventive and unique *Sky-Map of the Northern Hemisphere,* completed in 1515, shows an outsized circle representing the dark celestial sphere, or night sky. On its surface are displayed the principal constellations, shown in the mythical forms given to them by the classical Greeks and Romans. Heracles (Hercules) holds his signature symbols—a club and lion skin. Perseus flies along, carrying Medusa's severed head, while not far away loom the Argonauts Castor and Polydeuces (better known as Gemini, the twins).

WORD ORIGINS

constellation

In modern life: in astronomy, a group of stars that appear to form an image in the night sky.

In ancient Greece: *astron*, a group of stars that seemed to form an image in the night sky.

Italian master Benvenuto Cellini's 1554 bronze statue, Perseus with the Head of Medusa, *endures as a major tourist attraction more than four hundred years after its creation. Greek myths have inspired countless artists, musicians, and moviemakers, and will likely continue to do so in the centuries to come.*

The Heroes in Music

Like their literary counterparts, Western musical composers have often turned for inspiration to the Greek mythical heroes. The first musical work based on any of those characters was one of the earliest known operas—*Euridice* (1600), a version of the myth of the romantic hero Orpheus. No single composer created the entire work; rather, it was a joint effort of several members of the Camerata, an artistic society based in Florence.

Making the Great Bronze Perseus

Sixteenth-century Italian master Benvenuto Cellini's large bronze statue of Perseus, standing almost two stories high, is the world's most renowned sculpture of that well-known mythical character. The famous hero holds the head of the female monster Medusa while her hideous body limply sprawls at his feet. To create this magnificent work, Cellini began by collecting huge amounts of modeling clay and employing it to fashion clay models of Perseus and Medusa. He needed to ensure that the models contained every detail, no matter how small, that he desired to appear in the completed work. Thus, that step took far longer than any of the others. Next, Cellini erected a large iron framework to support the heavy clay. In his autobiography, he explains that he "covered the iron skeleton with clay, which I modeled like an anatomical subject." Next the sculptor carefully sliced the model into individual pieces and baked each in a big kiln. Once the hardened pieces had cooled, he covered them with wet plaster. When the plaster dried, he separated it from the clay, giving him negative, or recessed, molds of the positive clay pieces. Into the negative plaster molds, Cellini poured liquid wax, which dried into solid, positive wax replicas of the initial clay models. He then used a similar process to make bronze versions of the wax pieces. In the final last step, Cellini reassembled the individual bronze pieces, producing the finished statue, which he polished until it gleamed in the sunlight.

Benvenuto Cellini, *Autobiography,* trans. John A. Symonds. New York: Pocket, 1940, p. 442.

A number of later European operas deal with other famous Greek heroes. Italian composer Francesco Cavalli's *Jason* (1649), an opera about the title character's epic search for the Golden Fleece, was a notable example. English composer Henry Purcell's work *Dido and Aeneas* (ca. 1689) featured the renowned Greco-Roman hero Aeneas, who supposedly fled Troy after the Greeks sacked it, sailed to Italy, and there founded the Roman race.

In the twentieth century, another kind of stage show featuring singing—the American Broadway musical—became popular. The creators of that new medium also viewed the ancient Greek heroes as entertaining characters. One of the earliest Broadway hits, *By Jupiter* (1942), was based on one of Hercules's well-known twelve labors. A decade later *The Golden Apple* (1953) presented New York audiences with a melodic, moving tragic-comic version of the interplay among the heroes of the Trojan War. Later still, in 1975, *Home Sweet Homer* opened on Broadway. Based on Homer's *Odyssey*, it starred Oscar-winning actor Yul Brynner as the heroic Odysseus.

More recently, in 2008 noted American DJ Andy Butler produced a music album titled *Hercules and Love Affair*, performed by a musical group of the same name. Based on the Greek myth in which the famous strongman searches in vain for his lost young friend Hylas, the album reached the top-40 music listings in several countries. The group followed up with albums in 2011 and 2014. The music is presented in varied modern styles, including disco (pioneered in the 1970s), house (electronic dance music introduced in the 1980s), and nu-disco (popular into 2015).

> ## WORD ORIGINS
>
> ### authenticity
>
> In modern life: validity, genuineness, or proof of something's originality.
>
> In ancient Greece: *authentikos*, meaning original.

The Heroes on Film

The *Odyssey* and Hercules have also been the subjects of a number of movies, beginning with a silent French film, *Ulysses and the Giant Polyphemus*, in 1905. The first major sound version was a 1955 Italian production titled *Ulysses*, with noted American actor Kirk Douglas in the title role. More spectacular still was a 1997 television miniseries, *The Odyssey*, starring Armand Assante as Odysseus.

Still another movie about Odysseus's adventures appeared in 2008. Titled *Odysseus and the Isle of the Mists*, it was directed by Terry

Former professional wrestler Dwayne Johnson played the title character in the 2014 film Hercules. *More films have been made about Hercules than all of the other mythological Greek heroes combined, a testament to his enduring appeal.*

Ingram for the popular Syfy television channel. The story begins with a fictional account of the elderly epic poet Homer sitting down to add an extra section to his great work, the *Odyssey*, well after the initial version had become well known across Greece. In that supposedly newly discovered episode of his wanderings, Odysseus visits the Isle of the Mists, where he finds Persephone, wife of Hades, divine ruler of the underworld. That dark female figure turns out to be the mother of some vampire-like flying creatures similar to the Harpies in the Greek myths. In the end, Odysseus manages to escape and make it back to his homeland of Ithaca.

Movies about Hercules have been even more numerous than those about Odysseus and all of the other mythical Greek heroes combined. That is not surprising when one considers that Heracles/Hercules was by far the most popular legendary hero in the Greco-Roman world. Several silent and early sound films that featured him enjoyed varying degrees of success. American bodybuilder Steve Reeves starred in the 1957 Italian film *The Labors of Hercules,* which was released in the United States simply as *Hercules* in 1959. "No single film based on a Greek myth has been more influential," film historian Jon Solomon writes. Indeed, the movie cost $120,000 to make and raked in at least $18 million at the box office, turning films about the mythical strongman into a true craze. "In the next ten years," Solomon continues, "approximately twenty-five Hercules movies were released in bulging muscular-scope."[28] These mostly forgettable low-budget productions included *Hercules at the Center of the Earth* (1961), with Reg Park in the title role; *Hercules Against the Barbarians* (1964), with Mark Forest; and *Hercules in New York* (1969), with Arnold Schwarzenegger.

Several television series and live-action and animated movies about Hercules appeared in the decades that followed. Of those later Hercules productions, perhaps the most expensive and lavish was the 2014 3-D film *Hercules,* starring former professional wrestler Dwayne Johnson as the renowned strongman. The plot follows the great hero as he raises an army to defend the northern Greek region of Thrace from an invasion by an evil warlord. Predictably, Hercules eventually manages to save Thrace.

The many movies about the Greek heroes—together with poems, plays, novels, paintings, sculptures, operas, songs, television shows, comic books, and video games featuring those characters—have made them part of Western civilization's very fabric. Neither time nor the disappearance of the once great civilization that generated them has dulled the luster of their myths. It is almost certain, therefore, that those tales will remain compelling and popular for as long as people enjoy good storytelling. Edith Hamilton—herself a great myth-teller—aptly stated that the old heroic myths "have been proved by two thousand years, and more, to be immortal."[29]

Source Notes

Introduction: Tales from the Age of Heroes

1. Hesiod, *Theogony*, in *Hesiod, the Homeric Hymns, and Homerica*, trans. H.G. Evelyn-White. Cambridge, MA: Harvard University Press, 1964, p. 135.

2. Quoted in Euripides, *Alcestis*, in *Euripides: "Alcestis," "Hippolytus," "Iphigenia in Tauris,"* trans. Philip Vellacott. Baltimore: Penguin, 1968, p. 147.

3. John Camp and Elizabeth Fisher, *The World of the Ancient Greeks*. London: Thames and Hudson, 2002, pp. 60–61.

4. Philip Mayerson, *Classical Mythology in Literature, Art, and Music*. Newburyport, MA: R. Pullins, 2001, p. 280.

Chapter One: Champions of the Trojan War

5. Homer, *Iliad*. Book 9, lines 412–15, trans. Don Nardo.

6. C.M. Bowra, "Problems Concerned with Homer and the Epics," in *Homer's History: Mycenaean or Dark Age?*, ed. C.G. Thomas. New York: Holt, Rinehart and Winston, 1970, p. 9.

7. Plutarch, *Sayings of Spartan Women*, in *Plutarch on Sparta*, trans. Richard J.A. Talbert. New York: Penguin, 1988, p. 161.

8. Max J. Herzberg, *Myths and Their Meanings*. Boston: Allyn and Bacon, pp. 190–91.

9. Homer, *Iliad*. Book 22, lines 321–30, 331–36, trans. Don Nardo.

10. Arrian, *Anabasis Alexandri*. Book 5, section 26, trans. Don Nardo.

Chapter Two: Heroes on Epic Quests and Journeys

11. Edith Hamilton, *Mythology: Timeless Tales of Gods and Heroes*. New York: Grand Central, 2011, p. 17.

12. Homer, *Odyssey*. Book 9, lines 106–109, 115–17, trans. Don Nardo.

13. Homer, *Odyssey.* Book 9, lines 480–81, 398, trans. Don Nardo.

Chapter Three: Moving Tales of Heroic Lovers

14. Ovid, *Metamorphoses,* trans. Mary M. Innes. London: Penguin, 2006, p. 226.

15. Ovid, *Metamorphoses,* p. 226.

16. Quintus Smyrnaeus, *Fall of Troy,* trans. A.S. Way, in "Penthesilea," by Theoi Greek Mythology. www.theoi.com.

17. Madeline Miller, "Myth of the Week: Penthesilia." www.madelinemiller.com.

18. Aeschylus, *Seven Against Thebes,* in *Aeschylus: "Prometheus Bound," "The Suppliants," "Seven Against Thebes," "The Persians,"* trans. Philip Vellacott. Baltimore: Penguin, 1961, pp. 112–13.

19. Plato, *Symposium,* trans. Tom Griffith. Los Angeles: University of California Press, 1989, p. 27.

Chapter Four: Six Courageous Monster Slayers

20. Michael Grant, *Myths of the Greeks and Romans.* New York: New American Library, 1962, p. 45.

21. Joseph Campbell, *The Hero with a Thousand Faces.* Princeton, NJ: Princeton University Press, 1968, p. 30.

22. Plutarch, *Life of Theseus,* in *The Rise and Fall of Athens: Nine Greek Lives by Plutarch,* trans. Ian Scott-Kilvert. New York: Penguin, 1973, p. 24.

23. Plutarch, *Life of Theseus,* pp. 25–26.

24. John Mancini, "The Top Five Dragon-Slayers from Greek Mythology," Classical Wisdom Weekly. http://classicalwisdom.com.

25. Mancini, "The Top Five Dragon-Slayers from Greek Mythology."

26. Hamilton, *Mythology,* p. 161.

Chapter Five: Greek Heroes in Later Western Culture

27. Charlotte Coffin, "Shakespeare's Myths: Hercules," A Dictionary of Shakespeare's Classical Mythology, 2009. www.shakmyth.org.

28. Jon Solomon, *The Ancient World in the Cinema.* New Haven, CT: Yale University Press, 2001, pp. 117, 121.

29. Hamilton, *Mythology,* p. 5.

For Further Research

Books

Apollonius of Rhodes, *Argonautica*. Trans. Aaron Poochigian. New York: Penguin, 2014.

Jason Colavito, *Jason and the Argonauts Through the Ages*. Jefferson, NC: McFarland, 2014.

Michael Ford and Eoin Coveney, *Heroes, Gods, and Monsters of Ancient Greek Mythology*. St. Louis: Book House, 2015.

John H. Haaren and Addison B. Poland, *Four Heroes of Greek Mythology: Hercules, Jason, Achilles, and Ulysses*. New York: A.J. Cornell, 2011. Kindle edition.

Edith Hamilton, *Mythology: Timeless Tales of Gods and Heroes*. New York: Grand Central, 2011.

Emikos Kalyvas, *Theseus: The Hero of Athens*. Los Gatos, CA: Smashwords, 2015.

Charles Kingsley, *The Heroes*. Santa Barbara, CA: Mission Audio, 2011.

Mark P.O. Morford and Robert J. Lenardon, *Classical Mythology*. New York: Oxford University Press, 2010.

Karen R. Spies, *Heroes in Greek Mythology*. Berkeley Heights, NJ: Enslow, 2011.

Internet Sources

Kate Bernheimer, "Orpheus Through the Ages," *New Yorker*, October 15, 2013. www.newyorker.com/books/page-turner/orpheus-through -the-ages.

N.S. Gill, "The Ten Greatest Greek Heroes," About.com. http://an cienthistory.about.com/od/heroes/tp/TopHeroes.htm.

Manfred Korfmann, "Was There a Trojan War?," *Archaeology,* vol. 57, no. 3, May/June 2004. http://archive.archaeology.org/0405/etc/troy .html.

Vera Norman, "Four Conceptions of the Heroic," Fellowship of Reason. www.fellowshipofreason.com/archives/4heroes.htm.

Nick Squires, "Greeks Discover Odysseus' Palace in Ithaca, Proving Homer's Hero Was Real," *Telegraph,* August 2010. www.telegraph .co.uk/news/worldnews/europe/greece/7962445/Greeks-discover -Odysseus-palace-in-Ithaca-proving-Homers-hero-was-real.html.

Websites

Greek Mythology Link (www.maicar.com/GML/index.html). This well-thought-out site has a biographical dictionary with more than six thousand entries and some forty-five hundred photos, drawings, and other images.

Medea's Lair: Tales of Greek Mythology (www.medeaslair.net /myths.html). The authors of this site do a nice job of retelling the old myths, which are grouped into categories including "Men and Heroes," "Tales of Love and Loss," and "Giants and Beasts."

Mythweb Encyclopedia of Greek Mythology (www.mythweb.com /encyc). Although not as comprehensive and detailed as Theoi (see below), this website provides a lot of useful information about both major and minor Greek mythological characters.

Theoi Greek Mythology (http://www.theoi.com). This is the most comprehensive and reliable general website about Greek mythology on the Internet. It features hundreds of separate pages filled with detailed, accurate information as well as numerous primary sources.

Index

Picture Credits

Cover: iStockphoto.com

4: Maury Aaseng

6: Hercules and the Nemean Lion (oil on canvas), Rubens, Peter Paul (1577–1640) (after)/Apsley House, The Wellington Museum, London, UK/© Historic England/Bridgeman Images

14: Thetis giving Achilles his arms (fresco), Romano, Giulio (1492–1546) (and workshop)/Palazzo Ducale, Mantua, Italy/Bridgeman Images

17: akg-images/Newscom

20: He ran towards the horse and seized the bridle, illustration from 'The Story of Greece' by Mary Macgregor, 1st edition, 1913 (colour print), Crane, Walter (1845–1915)/Private Collection/The Stapleton Collection/Bridgeman Images

24: akg-images/Newscom

29: Depositphotos

33: © Christie's Images/Corbis

37: © Massimo Listri/Corbis

41: The Duel between Eteocles and Polynices, by Giovanni Silvagni, 1820, 19th Century, oil on canvas/Mondadori Portfolio/Electa/Giuseppe Schiavinotto/Bridgeman Images

45: © Stefano Bianchetti/Corbis

49: akg-images/Newscom

53: Cadmus and the dragon, 1938 (colour litho), Reid, Stephen (1873–1948)/Private Collection/Bridgeman Images

57: © Stefano Bianchetti/Corbis

61: © National Geographic Creative/Corbis

65: Depositphotos

68: Photofest Images

About the Author

Classical historian Don Nardo has written numerous acclaimed volumes about ancient civilizations and peoples. They include more than a dozen overviews of the mythologies of the Sumerians, Babylonians, Egyptians, Greeks, Romans, Persians, and others. Nardo also composes and arranges orchestral music. He lives with his wife, Christine, in Massachusetts.